MAGIC
Vegetable

by
Sheilah Kaufman

The
AMERICAN
★ COOKING ★
GUILD™

Boynton Beach, Florida

Dedication
For my parents, Leon and Reggie Weinraub.

Acknowledgments
—Edited by Martina Boudreau
—Cover Design and Layout by Pearl & Associates, Inc.
—Cover Photo by Burwell and Burwell
—Illustrations by Jean Brill Hough

More...Quick Recipes for Creative Cooking!
The American Cooking Guild's *Collector's Series* includes over 30 popular cooking topics such as Barbeque, Breakfast & Brunches, Chicken, Cookies, Hors d' Oeuvres, Seafood, Tea, Coffee, Pasta, Pizza, Salad, Italian and many more. Each book contains more than 50 selected recipes. For a catalog of these and many other full sized cookbooks, send $1 to the address below and a coupon will be included for $1 off your first order.

Cookbooks Make Great Premiums!
The American Cooking Guild has been the premier publisher of private label and custom cookbooks since 1981. Retailers, manufacturers, and food companies have all chosen The American Cooking Guild to publish their premium and promotional cookbooks. For further information on our special markets programs please contact the address.

The American Cooking Guild
3600-K South Congress Avenue
Boynton Beach, FL 33426

Table of Contents

Jean Hough

Introduction

Vegetables are the bounty of nature's production. There are many varieties in each of the "families," and that which we think of as vegetables frequently overlap with fruit (like tomatoes). Many vegetables are typically eaten raw and are delicious as such.

However, cooking can enhance the flavor of many vegetables, as well as making their use more versatile and increasing the ways of combining several vegetables for mutual flavor enhancement. Also, cooking certain vegetables swells and bursts the starch cells so that the center becomes soft and digestible. Cooking also breaks up fiber so that it can be used more efficiently by the body.

Although vegetables are frequently the "quick and simple" element of a meal, just steamed and served with butter or lemon juice, this cookbook is different. It offers many possibilities to make the vegetable the main course or even the dessert! It is unique in another respect—leftover steamed vegetables can be used in several dishes; or you'll be able to find a way to cook those carrots in the vegetable bin waiting to be stars.

Storing

When buying summer vegetables, buy only what you can use immediately, as they deteriorate very quickly. Winter vegetables can be bought in larger amounts and kept in a cool dry place.

Washing

Greens should be washed several times to remove all dirt; broccoli, cauliflower and brussels sprouts need to be soaked in salt water to get rid of all insects; and vegetables can be crisped by placing them in cold water.

Artichokes Stuffed with Asparagus

> 8 large artichokes
> 2 Tablespoons lemon juice
> 1½ pounds fresh asparagus
> 2 Tablespoons butter
> 2 Tablespoons cream
> 1 teaspoon lemon juice
>   salt, to taste
>   freshly ground pepper, to taste
>   big dash of Tabasco

Remove stems from artichokes. Trim the tips of the leaves with a scissors. Cut artichokes about ¾ of the way through, starting at top, so the choke is exposed.

Place artichokes in boiling salted water with 2 Tablespoons lemon juice. Cover and simmer about 30-45 minutes. Drain well. Cook asparagus in boiling salted water until tender. Drain well and place in blender or food processor and begin to puree. Add butter, cream, 1 teaspoon lemon juice, salt, pepper and Tabasco. Puree thoroughly. Place in a small pan and heat until hot.

Preheat oven to 350°(F).

Remove choke from artichokes, leaving bottom exposed, and fill with puree, mounding with a spoon. Arrange filled artichokes in oven-proof casserole, and heat in oven for 5 minutes, until warm.

Serves 8.

HINT: Fresh artichokes should be plump, compact, and heavy for their size. Leaves should be tightly closed, thick and green. Rub two artichokes together. If they squeak, they're fresh.

Asparagus Soup

1 Tablespoon butter
1 small onion, finely chopped
1 Tablespoon flour
4 cups chicken broth
  salt, to taste
  freshly ground pepper, to taste
1 pound fresh asparagus, washed and cut into
  small pieces
  juice and grated rind of 1 lemon

In a large pot, melt butter and stir in onions. Cook for about 3 minutes. Stir in flour. Whisk it well and stir continuously.

Add chicken broth gradually, stirring constantly. Add salt, pepper, and asparagus. Simmer, uncovered, for 20 minutes.

Puree soup in a blender. Strain blended soup into a clean pan, stir in lemon juice. Heat or chill. Serve hot or cold, garnished with grated lemon rind.

Serves 6.

HINT: Young, slim asparagus stalks are the most tender. Tips should be tightly closed. Before cooking, break the white end off—it breaks naturally at the edible part.

Asparagus Rollups

20 slices very soft white bread, with crusts removed
1 package (8 ounces) cream cheese, softened
4 ounces Bleu cheese, crumbled
1 egg
   dash of Tabasco sauce
   dash of Worcestershire sauce
1 pound fresh asparagus, steamed
   drained
½ cup melted butter or margarine

Flatten bread out by rolling each slice once or twice with a rolling pin.

In a small bowl, combine cheeses, egg, and Tabasco and Worcestershire sauces.

Spread this mixture evenly on each slice of bread.

Place one asparagus spear on each slice of bread, and roll up. If the spears are longer than the slices of bread, trim off the "overhang," and use 3 or 4 such extra pieces to fill one slice of bread.

Dip each piece of rolled-up bread in the melted butter, and slice into thirds. If not serving right away, rollups can be frozen at this point and reheated using the regular baking directions below.

Place slices on an ungreased cookie sheet.

Bake rollups at 425°(F) for 15 minutes, or until golden. Serve hot.

Makes 5 dozen.

Beets in Yogurt Sauce

1 Tablespoon chopped onion
1 Tablespoon olive or sunflower oil
2⅔ cups cooked and diced beets (preferably baked)
1 Tablespoon wholewheat flour
½ teaspoon ground cumin
3 Tablespoons chopped parsley
  salt to taste
  freshly ground pepper to taste
1 cup plain yogurt

Fry onion in oil until transparent, add beets and stir gently until thoroughly heated and beginning to fry. Sprinkle with flour, cumin and two-thirds of the parsley and season with salt and pepper.

Mix well, then pour on the yogurt and stir over moderate heat until mixture thickens.

Reduce heat and simmer for a few moments longer before serving. Sprinkle with remaining parsley.

Serves 4.

Broccoli and Cheese Fritters

Great recipe from the Carriage Club Restaurant at the Viscount Hotel in Miami.

> 2 cups all purpose flour
> 3 eggs
> 1 cup milk
> 1 Tablespoon baking powder
> 1½ teaspoons salt
> ½ teaspoon Worcestershire sauce
> 2 drops Tabasco
> 2 cups broccoli florets (cooked, cooled, and drained well)
> 1 cup coarsely grated sharp cheddar cheese
> oil for frying
> sweet and sour sauce (your favorite recipe)

Mix together flour, eggs, milk, baking powder, salt, Worcestershire, and Tabasco. Gently fold in broccoli and cheese.

Heat enough oil to cover the bottom of the skillet or fry pan and drop batter by spoonsful into oil. Turn once, cooking until golden brown.

Serve with sweet and sour sauce for dipping.

Makes 12 fritters; serves 2 for main course, 6 for appetizer.

Broccoli with Red Pepper

1   *bunch broccoli*
5   *Tablespoons oil*
1 or 2   *large cloves garlic, peeled*
freshly ground pepper
1 - 2   *Tablespoons red pepper flakes (crushed red*
pepper)
cold water

Remove stalks from broccoli and cut the remainder into 1½" pieces. Heat oil in a large skillet and add garlic cloves. Stir and cook on medium heat for about 2 minutes.

Remove garlic and discard it. Add broccoli, ground pepper, and flakes. Stir, then cover and cook over low heat.

If necessary, add a little cold water. Stir occasionally, and cook, covered, for about 15 minutes, or until the broccoli is completely cooked and soft.

Serves 4 - 6.

HINT: Broccoli buds are freshest when tightly closed; the tips may be tinged with blue or purple.

Brussels Sprouts in Sour Cream Sauce

Just the right flavor combination as a side dish for chicken, or white-fleshed fish.

> 1 pound fresh, small brussels sprouts
> (or 2 pkgs. frozen)
> ¼ cup chopped onion
> 2 Tablespoons butter
> 1 cup sour cream

Either steam brussels sprouts 10 minutes until tender, which preserves more of the vitamins and flavor, or cook as package directs. Drain well.

Sauté onion in butter, add sour cream and heat just until warm—do not boil or it will curdle. Add sprouts and mix well.

Serve warm.
Serves 4 - 6.

HINT: Brussels sprouts, a member of the cabbage family, are bite-sized, round-headed and tightly closed. Although the outer leaves are green to dark green, the inner core is very pale-almost white.

To prepare, scrape off the stem with a sharp knife. Cut an "X" in the stem to speed cooking time.

Layered Red Cole Slaw

1 red cabbage, shredded
1 onion, sliced thin
1 green pepper, sliced
¾ cup sugar
1 cup cider vinegar
1 teaspoon salt
½ teaspoon celery seed
1 teaspoon dry mustard
¾ cup oil

In a large bowl, layer cabbage, onion and green pepper. Pour sugar over vegetables but do not mix. Combine cider vinegar, salt, celery seed, dry mustard, and oil in a pan. Bring to a boil. Pour over vegetables, but do not mix. Cover and refrigerate overnight. Toss and serve.
Serves 8 - 10.

HINT: Pick cabbages with bright color. They should be firm and feel heavy for their size. These are one of the best "keepers"—stored in a plastic bag in your refrigerator's crisper, they will keep for weeks.

Sweet & Sour Carrots

   3 *pounds carrots, peeled and cut into 1½-inch*
      strips
   1 *can (10¾ ounces) tomato soup, undiluted*
   1 *cup cider vinegar*
   1 *cup sugar*
1½ *cups salad oil*
   1 *teaspoon dry mustard*
   1 *green pepper, finely chopped*
   1 *medium onion, finely chopped*

The day before serving, bring 4 quarts of salted water to a boil in a large kettle.

Add carrots, and cook until tender but not too soft.

Drain carrots well.

In a large glass or plastic bowl, combine the remaining ingredients, mixing well.

Add carrots, mixing until they are well coated with the marinade.

Cover the bowl and refrigerate the carrots overnight, longer if desired.

Serves 10 - 12.

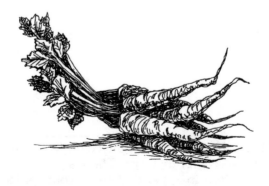

Carrots Divine

Make in a ring mold or a souffle dish. Tastes great! This recipe can be doubled or tripled. It's like a carrot spoonbread.

          10 carrots, peeled
           2 teaspoons lemon juice
         1⅔ sticks butter or margarine
          ¼ cup Crisco®
          ½ cup dark brown sugar
           1 egg
           1 cup flour
           1 teaspoon baking powder
           1 teaspoon baking soda

Preheat oven to 350º(F). Boil carrots until soft enough to mash. Drain and mash and sprinkle with lemon juice.

Cream together margarine, Crisco, brown sugar and egg. Add flour, baking powder and baking soda. Mix well. Add mashed carrots, blending well.

Pour into slightly greased mold, souffle (2 qt) or 8½" x 4½" loaf pan. Bake for 50 - 60 minutes. Unmold and serve when warm. Can be frozen and reheated in foil.

Serves 6.

HINT: Carrots stay fresh longer than many other vegetables, especially if refrigerated.

Polly Clingerman's Cauliflower Delux

Polly is a noted hostess and cook in Washington, D.C.

> 2 cups yogurt (or cream)
> ½ cup chopped onion
> 1½ teaspoons ground ginger
> 1½ teaspoons garlic powder
> ¼ teaspoon turmeric
> ½ teaspoon salt
> ¼ teaspoon cinnamon
> seeds of 1 cardamom
> 2 cloves
> ¾ teaspoon cornstarch
> 3 Tablespoons oil
> 2 bay leaves
> ¼ teaspoon black mustard seeds
> ¼ teaspoon cumin seeds
> 1 cauliflower
> 1 Tablespoon chopped fresh coriander (optional)
> 1 peeled, seeded, chopped tomato

Combine yogurt, onion, ginger, garlic powder, turmeric, salt, cinnamon, cardamom, cloves and cornstarch in a blender for 3 minutes. In a skillet, heat oil, add bay leaves, mustard seed, and cumin. Cook, stirring, for 2 minutes.

Parboil cauliflower for 5 minutes, drain and cut off stalk, leaving bunches of flowers. Add to spice and oil mixture. Cook until golden. Add coriander. Add blender mixture, cover and simmer on low, stirring occasionally, for 3 - 5 minutes. Stir in tomato, cover and simmer another 3 - 5 minutes.

Serves 6.

London Cauliflower

1 *fresh-picked cauliflower*
2 *Tablespoons butter*
1 *Tablespoon chopped fresh chives*
1 *Tablespoon chopped fresh parsley*
  salt and pepper to taste

Select a mature head of cauliflower from the garden, with fresh green leaves. Clean and wash, leaving two rows of leaves surrounding the head.

Steam cauliflower until just tender. Place on a hot serving platter.

Melt butter, blend in seasonings and pour over the cauliflower.

Serve at once.

Serves 4 - 6.

Iowa Corn Pancakes

2 cups corn kernels, drained if using canned
¼ cup flour
½ teaspoon baking powder
½ teaspoon sugar
½ teaspoon salt
   pinch of nutmeg
   dash of Tabasco
¼ cup whipping cream
2 eggs
2 Tablespoons margarine or butter

Place the corn, flour, baking powder, sugar, salt, nutmeg, Tabasco, whipping cream and eggs in a blender or processor. Blend or process for about 15 seconds or until well-blended.

Refrigerate mixture for at least an hour. In a small skillet or on a griddle, melt margarine. When hot, drop large spoonsful of pancake mixture to form 2" rounds. Cook until top looks dry and edges begin to brown. Turn and cook briefly on the other side. Serve immediately.

Repeat with remaining batter.
Makes 12 - 14 pancakes.

Cahn's Peanut Buttered Corn

1 stick margarine, room temperature
1 Tablespoon peanut butter
   pinch of curry powder (to taste)
   pinch of salt
   corn on the cob

Cream margarine with peanut butter, curry and salt. Use like butter or margarine on boiled corn on the cob, or rub on raw corn on the cob and wrap it in aluminum foil and roast in the oven or on the grill.
Will cover 4 - 8 ears.

Gould's Fried Corn on the Cob

1 egg
1 Tablespoon milk
1 teaspoon chicken bouillon powder (or 1 cube)
½ cup all-purpose flour
   salt to taste
   pepper to taste
   dash cayenne
4 ears corn on cob, cleaned
   oil for frying

Combine egg, milk, and bouillon, in a bowl. In another bowl, combine flour, salt, pepper and cayenne.

Dip corn in egg mixture and then in flour mixture. Deep fry in hot oil (around 375º(F)) until golden brown.

Drain on paper towel and serve.

Serves 4.

HINT: Everyone with a garden patch knows that you have the pot boiling before you dash out to pick the corn for dinner. If there's a longer delay, look for fresh-looking green husks; silk should be golden brown, not very dark, but slightly dark, not dry. Kernels should be plump, popping with juice—not tough or dry.

Anna Meyer's Cucumber Delight

A recipe right from Grandmother that's still popular, but even more so than it was years ago.

> 4 - 5 cucumbers peeled and sliced thin
> ½ small onion sliced thin (or use a Spanish onion)
> 2 teaspoons sugar
> ¼ cup cider vinegar
> freshly ground pepper
> salt to taste
> ½ cup whipping cream (or more)

Combine all ingredients except the cream. Add enough cream (or cream mixed with milk) to cover. Cover with foil and refrigerate overnight. More cucumbers can be added as needed, and the taste (sweet and sour) can be adjusted to suit your tastebuds!

Serves 8 - 10.

HINT: Looking for a perfect cucumber? Select one that is long, lean and well-shaped. The green skin should never be yellowing or look "puffy"—a sign of overripeness and mushy texture.

Cucumbers Hungarian

2 *large cucumbers*
¼ *cup sour cream*
3 *Tablespoons mayonnaise*
3 *teaspoons paprika**
¾ *teaspoon sugar*
3 *teaspoons lemon juice*
salt
freshly ground pepper to taste

Peel cucumbers and cut in half lengthwise. Scoop out the seeds and slice cucumbers into thin slices.

Combine remaining ingredients and toss with cucumbers. Chill well before serving.

Serves 4.

*It is important that your paprika is fresh. As with all red spices, keep your paprika in the refrigerator.

Japanese Cucumber-Shrimp Salad

1 large cucumber
½ teaspoon salt
3 Tablespoons white wine vinegar
2 Tablespoons sugar
1 teaspoon peeled and thinly sliced fresh ginger root
¼ cup finely chopped cooked shrimp

Peel cucumber and cut in half lengthwise. Scrape out and discard seeds. Cut cucumber into thin slices. Place slices in a bowl, sprinkle with ¼ teaspoon salt, toss and let sit 30 minutes.

Prepare dressing by combining vinegar, sugar, ¼ teaspoon salt. Stir until dry ingredients are dissolved.

Drain cucumber, pressing the slices to release all their liquid. Add sliced ginger root and pour dressing over all. Toss to mix well.

Serve garnished with chopped shrimp.

Serves 4.

Eggplant or Green Beans
in Garlic Sauce

Will make anyone a vegetable lover!

> 2 *medium eggplants or 1 pound fresh green string beans*
> 6 *garlic cloves, minced*
> 2 · 3 *Tablespoons chili paste with garlic*
> 4 *Tablespoons dark soy sauce*
> 2 *Tablespoons black vinegar*
> 2 *Tablespoons sugar*
> ½ *cup or more peanut oil*
> ¼ *pound ground hamburger or pork*
> 1½ *cups diced scallions*

Cut eggplant into 3"x ¾" strips, but don't peel. (If using beans, cut off ends and cut beans in half). Combine minced garlic with chili paste.

In another bowl, mix soy sauce, vinegar and sugar. Heat wok over medium heat, and add one third of the oil. As soon as oil gets hot, add half eggplant or beans and stir-fry until eggplant begins to brown. Remove to a platter and repeat with remaining eggplant or beans.

Add 3 more tablespoons oil to the wok and when hot add the garlic-chili paste mixture. Stir for about 12 seconds and add ground meat. Stir until meat is lightly browned.

Re-add eggplant or beans and stir to mix well. Add scallions and stir another half minute. Add soy-vinegar mixture and stir for a minute.

Serve immediately. If the meat is left out, this dish can be made ahead and served cold.

Serves 4 - 6.

HINT: Be sure to select garlic with clean, unbroken skins. Bulbs should be plump and hard. Store in a cool, dry place, where air can circulate freely.

Scalloped Eggplant

1 large eggplant, firm with no soft spots
6 slices bacon
3 eggs
1 cup milk
2 cups cubed white bread without crusts
1 cup grated Cheddar cheese
1 Tablespoon butter
¼ cup grated Parmesan for topping

Cut eggplant into 1" square cubes, and par-boil in boiling water. Drain the eggplant cubes well, patting dry with paper towels.

Fry bacon slices until the fat is rendered out, and cut bacon into one inch pieces.

Beat eggs, add milk and combine with eggplant, bacon, and bread cubes.

Mix in grated Cheddar; pour into buttered 2 quart casserole, (you may need a larger one), dot with butter, and sprinkle with Parmesan.

Bake at 325°(F) until set and browned—usually about 30-40 minutes.

Serves 4 - 6.

HINT: Boiling eggplant prior to using it in a casserole helps to remove the bitter-tasting black liquid. This process will give it a gentle, rich quality without spoiling its "nutty" flavor.

Indian Eggplant

1 eggplant
3 Tablespoons oil
4 small chopped onions
1 teaspoon cumin seed
1 teaspoon salt
½ teaspoon chili powder
1 - 2 teaspoons coriander powder
1 Tablespoon tomato paste
6 Tablespoons water

Place a cake rack on stove burner on high heat. Cook eggplant on each side until blistered and burnt. Peel and rinse in cold water.

Saute the chopped onions in oil. Add spices, tomato paste and water. Stir and cook. Mash eggplant and add, reducing heat to low. Cook 15 - 20 minutes.

Should be slightly runny.

Serves 4 - 6.

HINT: Shiny, firm, rich purple eggplants that appear heavy for their size are prime quality for eating. If there is too much of a green undertone, the eggplant isn't quite ripe; wrinkled, flabby eggplant is overripe and tastes bitter.

Baked Fennel Parmesan

For a refreshing change of taste in vegetables.

 3 *heads fennel*
 2 *cups milk*
 ½ *onion, sliced*
 2 *quarts water*
   freshly ground pepper
   salt
 2 *teaspoons butter or margarine*
 ¾ - 1 *cup freshly grated Parmesan cheese*
 2 *Tablespoons bread crumbs*
 1 *Tablespoon olive oil*

Trim fennel, but leave it whole. Preheat oven to 425º(F).

In a pan over medium heat, bring the milk, onion, and water to a boil. Add fennel. Reduce heat to simmer and cook until tender. Drain well, but save ¼ cup cooking liquid.

Trim, halve and core the fennel. Place in a buttered baking dish, and sprinkle with pepper and salt to taste. Dot the top with butter or margarine and sprinkle with Parmesan, bread crumbs and reserved cooking liquid.

Place in oven until heated through. Drizzle with olive oil and serve.

Serves 6 - 8.

HINT: Fennel is sometimes labeled "anise" by the grocery store's produce manager. It is most widely available in late fall and early winter.

Green Bean Mousse

A novel way to serve an ordinary vegetable. The texture is that of a souffle.

> 1 *pound fresh green beans*
> ¼ *cup whipping cream*
> 4 *egg yolks*
> *pinch of nutmeg*
> *freshly ground pepper*
> *salt*
> 1 *Tablespoon butter*

Preheat oven to 350º(F).

Cook beans in boiling, salted water for 5 - 10 minutes. Drain and rinse well.

In the blender or food processor, combine the beans, cream, egg yolks, nutmeg, salt and pepper.

Butter a 1 - 1½ quart souffle dish. Place in pan of boiling water. Pour in batter.

Bake for 20 minutes, covered with foil.

Serves 6 - 8.

HINT: Green beans should be crisp and tender, without scars; they should have a pliable, velvety feel.

Green Beans Au Gratin

1 pound fresh green beans, cleaned and blanched
8 slices bacon, fried until crisp
1 cup shredded cheddar cheese
1½ cups light cream
½ teaspoon salt
   freshly ground pepper to taste
   nutmeg
3 eggs, slightly beaten

Preheat oven to 375°(F).

Drain beans. Place in shallow, buttered baking dish. Crumble cooked bacon over the beans. Sprinkle with the Cheddar cheese.

Combine cream, salt, pepper, nutmeg and eggs. Mix well Pour over beans.

Bake for 25 minutes.

Serves 6.

Braised Kohlrabi

1½ pounds kohlrabi, trimmed and peeled
2 Tablespoons margarine
¼ cup chicken stock or broth
1 teaspoon fresh, minced tarragon
   salt
   freshly ground pepper
¼ cup fresh, chopped parsley

Cut the kohlrabi bulbs into 3" long strips about ¼" wide.

In a large skillet over medium heat, melt margarine and add the strips. Stir to toss and coat them. Stir in chicken broth and tarragon. Cover and cook until tender, about 15 minutes.

Remove the cover and continue cooking until golden.

Add salt and pepper to taste and sprinkle with parsley just before serving.

Serves 4 - 6.

HINT: Kohlrabi in its young, most tender stage has a bulb diameter of less than 3 inches. It is one of the most mild-tasting members of the cabbage family. Wash and trim just before cooking.

Leek & Clam Chowder Christensen

8 large chowder clams
2 cups boiling water
1 bunch leeks (at least 6 large, without green)
2 medium potatoes, peeled and cubed
2 cloves garlic, finely chopped
¼ cup sweet yellow sherry
¼ cup whipping cream
2 Tablespoons butter
  salt
  freshly ground pepper

Scrub dirt and sand from clams. Place in a large pot of boiling water.

When clams open, remove from heat and dice meat after removing from shells. Discard shells. Set aside to cool, but save cooking liquid.

Chop leeks and place in clam liquid. Add potatoes, garlic and sherry. Bring to boil, reduce heat and simmer, covered, for about 10 minutes or until potatoes are soft. Remove from heat and cool, strain off broth and set aside.

Puree mixture in blender, adding enough broth to give desired consistency. Add whipping cream, butter, salt, and pepper to taste. Add diced clams.

Can be carefully reheated, but doesn't freeze well with potatoes.

Serves 6 - 8.

HINT: Leeks need special attention to remove all the grit. First, cut off the fibrous leaf tops and the root base. Slip a knife through the leek where the white and green parts meet, and draw the knife all the way through the leaves. Slit again at a right angle to the first cut. Rinse the leek in a bowl of cold water until there is no more grit.

Tossed Italian Salad

> 5 cups Iceberg or Romaine lettuce
> ½ pounds fresh mushrooms, sliced
> 4 ounces Mozzarella cheese, cut in rectangles
> 1 cup drained garbanzo beans
> ½ cup thinly sliced pepperoni
> ½ cup Italian salad dressing
> wine vinegar, to taste

The night before serving, place lettuce in a baggie with ice cubes. Tie it shut. Place mushrooms, sliced cheese, garbanzo beans and sliced pepperoni in a baggie and tie it shut.

Before serving, pour the water off lettuce and add vegetable-cheese-pepperoni mixture. Add dressing and wine vinegar, if desired.

Shake everything in the baggie and pour into a serving bowl.

Serves 6-8.

Connie's Salad

From Connie to my friend Ellen to me, and is well worth trying!

>   1 head Romaine lettuce
>   1 red Bermuda onion, sliced
>   ½ cup mayonnaise
>   2 Tablespoons white vinegar
>   ¼ cup sugar
>   ⅓ cup milk
>   1 pint strawberries, sliced

Place Romaine leaves in a large bowl and toss with onion slices.

Whisk together the mayonnaise, vinegar, sugar and milk.

Add strawberries and pour over salad before serving.
Serves 4 - 6.

Russian Mushrooms

1 pound fresh mushrooms
¼ cup butter
2 Tablespoons finely chopped shallots or green
   onions
   dash of salt
1 teaspoon paprika
1 Tablespoon flour
¼ cup white wine
1 cup sour cream

In a heated sauté pan, sauté mushrooms in butter with onion at medium heat. Be careful to keep heat constant, or mushrooms will "render their juices" before the onion is soft. Add salt and paprika.

Add flour (sprinkle over the mixture evenly) and cook 1 minute longer. Add wine, continue cooking and add sour cream. Bring just to boiling point, but do not let boil.

Serve on toast or English muffins—the thinner sliced toast is better.

Serves 2 - 4.

HINT: To cook mushrooms, first clean by wiping off dirt with a dampened paper towel. Do not soak, as mushrooms will absorb moisture and become soggy. Cut off tips of stems, and proceed with your recipe.

Mushroom Turnovers

> 1 *favorite double piecrust recipe*
> ¼ *cup butter, softened*
> 2 *Tablespoons butter*
> ½ *cup finely chopped onion*
> ¼ *pound fresh mushrooms, chopped*
> 1 *teaspoon flour*
> ½ *teaspoon garlic salt*
> ¼ *teaspoon dried thyme*
>   *dash cayenne*
> 1 *egg yolk*

Preheat oven to 400º(F).

Make your favorite piecrust recipe (doubled). Shape into a ball and roll out on lightly floured surface to a 12"x 16" rectangle. Spread with the softened butter to ½" from the edges.

Fold lengthwise into thirds. Press edges together to seal. Then starting at one end, fold into thirds. Wrap in wax paper and refrigerate at least one hour. Butter should be firm.

In a large skillet, melt 2 tablespoons butter and sauté onion until golden. Add mushrooms and sauté 3 minutes. Remove from heat. Stir in flour and seasonings. Cook, stirring, for 1 minute or until mixture is thickened. Place in a small bowl, cover and refrigerate for 1 hour.

Divide pastry in half. Roll out on lightly floured surface, into an 11" square. Cut into 16 rounds, using a 2½" cookie cutter. Place 1 teaspoon of filling on half of each round. Fold the other half of dough over the filling and press edge with a fork to seal. Repeat with remaining dough and filling.

Beat egg yolk with 1 tablespoon water. Place turnovers on ungreased cookie sheet and brush with egg yolk mixture.

Bake at 400º(F) for 15 - 20 minutes or until golden brown.

Makes 32 turnovers; serves 10 - 12 as an appetizer.

Duxelles

Great as a stuffing or filling for veal, chicken or fish.

> ¼ *cup finely chopped shallots*
> 4 *Tablespoons unsalted butter*
> 1 *pound fresh mushrooms, finely chopped*
> ¼ *cup dry white wine*
> 1 *teaspoon salt*
> *freshly ground pepper*
> *pinch of freshly grated nutmeg*
> 2 *Tablespoons chopped fresh parsley*

In a skillet, over medium heat, sauté shallots in butter for 5 minutes. Add mushrooms, wine, salt, pepper, and nutmeg, and cook for 10 minutes, stirring, or until all moisture has evaporated from the mixture. Add parsley, stir and remove from heat.

Let cool. Then store in refrigerator, covered, or seal and freeze for later use.

HINT: Mushrooms do not keep well, so buy them no more than a day or two before using. Pick mushrooms with unblemished skins. Refrigerate, unwashed, until cooking time.

French Fried Okra

Okra has become a "gourmet" vegetable, but it has been a southern staple forever. This recipe will remind you a little of popcorn. It is easily doubled.

> 1 pound fresh, young okra
> 1 egg, beaten
>   dash Tabasco sauce
>   dash Worcestershire sauce
> 1 teaspoon garlic salt (or to taste)
>   white cornmeal (or yellow)
>   cooking oil
>   salt

Cut ends off okra and slice into "coins" about ⅜-inches in diameter. Par-boil for a few minutes, and rinse.

Beat egg in a bowl with flavorings. Dip okra first into egg, then into cornmeal, completely covering okra. Fry in oil until golden brown (not too brown)*. Remove and sprinkle with salt. Drain on paper towels.

Taste one or two pieces to check for proper seasoning.
Serves 4 - 6.

*Test a few unbreaded okra in your oil first, to make sure the oil is at proper frying temperature.

Okra-Zucchini Delight

> 6 strips bacon
> 6 small okra
> 1 small green pepper
> 1 medium onion, chopped
> 2½ cups zucchini, coarsely chopped
> 4 Tablespoons tomato paste
>   pinch of thyme
>   salt
>   freshly ground pepper
> ½ cup grated Parmesan cheese

Preheat oven to 350º(F).

Cook bacon in a skillet. When crisp and done, remove from skillet and chop. Save a little of the bacon fat in the skillet.

Slice okra thin and chop green pepper. In the remaining bacon fat, saute chopped onion until golden, then add chopped zucchini, green pepper, okra, tomato paste, chopped bacon, thyme, salt and pepper. Cook mixture until zucchini is tender.

Place in an ovenproof dish and cover with grated Parmesan cheese.

Bake until cheese is melted and browned.

Serves 4 - 6.

Honey Baked Onions

6 medium Bermuda onions
3 Tablespoons honey
2 Tablespoons margarine
salt
freshly ground pepper

Preheat oven to 350º(F).

Slice an area off of the bottom of onions, so they sit flat. Peel onions and prick several times with a fork. Place onions in an ovenproof casserole with a tight-fitting lid. Drizzle with honey and dot with margarine; sprinkle with salt and pepper.

Cook for 1 - 1½ hours, or until onions are tender.

Serves 6.

HINT: The best onions are dry, firm and dirt-free, with a brittle skin. Bermudas are best in March. Onions like to be stored in a cool, dark place; the damp air of a refrigerator encourages rot.

Sweet & Sour Onions

1½ pounds small white onions (or frozen ones)
½ stick margarine
1 teaspoon salt
3 Tablespoons dark brown sugar
3 Tablespoons red wine vinegar

Place onions in boiling water for about 3 minutes or cook according to package directions. In a skillet, melt margarine and add onions. Stir over medium heat and add salt. Cook for 5 minutes and then add sugar and red wine vinegar. Cook another 5 minutes.

Best to prepare this the day before and serve hot.
Serves 6 - 8.

Peas in Sour Cream Dill Sauce

> 1 pound tiny peas, cooked and drained
> 1 cup sour cream
> ½ cup fresh dill, chopped
>   salt
>   freshly ground pepper
> 1 teaspoon curry powder

Combine sour cream and all spices in a bowl and mix well with the peas. Chill several hours before serving.
Serves 4 - 6.

HINT: The smaller the pea pod, the more tender the pea. Fresh peas squeak when the pods are rubbed together. Fresh peas are best used as soon as possible after purchasing.

Pea, Tomato and Rice Salad

1 cup green peas, cooked
2 tomatoes, peeled, seeded and chopped
2 cups hot, cooked rice
¾ cup olive oil
3 Tablespoons vinegar
salt
freshly ground pepper
⅓ cup finely chopped fresh parsley
1 Tablespoon fresh basil, finely chopped

Mix peas and tomatoes together.

While rice is still hot from cooking, toss with olive oil, vinegar, salt and pepper. Cool.

Add peas and tomatoes, parsley and basil. Mix well and chill thoroughly.

Serves 4 - 6.

Chinese Chicken with Snow Peas

3 *Tablespoons soy sauce*
2 *Tablespoons cornstarch*
2 *Tablespoons dry white sherry*
4 *chicken breasts cut into bite-size pieces*
oil
6 *ounces Chinese snow peas*
½ *pound fresh mushrooms, sliced thin*
salt
freshly ground pepper

Combine soy sauce, cornstarch and sherry in a bowl. Place chicken pieces in soy mixture and mix well. Let sit about 20 - 30 minutes.

In a wok, heat 2 or 3 tablespoons oil until hot. Toss in marinated chicken, a handful at a time, and stir over medium high heat for about 3 minutes, or until chicken is done. Push pieces up the sides of the wok or remove to a plate. Repeat until all chicken is cooked. Add more oil if necessary, and let heat.

Stir in snow peas and sliced mushrooms. Add salt and pepper. Mix in cooked chicken and stir until everything is hot.

Serve with rice.

Serves 2 - 3.

HINT: Snow peas are a bright green and so thin you can see the immature peas within. Since they are eaten for their pod, select tender, sweet snow peas, and prepare as soon as possible.

Marinated Peppers
and Montrachet Cheese

Best made early in the day, or the day before, this flavorful combination can serve as either appetizer or salad.

> 6 *ounces Montrachet or other mild, log-shaped*
> *goat cheese*
> 1 *Tablespoon fresh rosemary, chopped (or 1*
> *teaspoon, dried and crushed)*
> 5 *Tablespoons extra-virgin olive oil*
> 2 *red sweet peppers*
> 2 *yellow sweet peppers*
> 1 *clove garlic, minced*
> *freshly ground black pepper*
> *Radicchio or Bibb lettuce leaves*

Slice cheese into ¾-inch rounds and arrange in small, shallow dish. Sprinkle evenly with rosemary and drizzle with 3 tablespoons of olive oil. Cover and marinate several hours or overnight in refrigerator.

Meanwhile, preheat broiler. Wash peppers and place on broiler pan about 2" from flame. Roast 15 to 20 minutes, turning occasionally so that all sides blister and char evenly. (Watch yellow peppers carefully; the flesh burns easily.) Place in plastic bag and seal until cool enough to handle.

Slip off skins, cut away stem and remove seeds. Slice into very thin strips and place in small bowl. Add garlic, remaining olive oil and pepper to taste and toss to coat well. Marinate several hours or overnight.

To serve, bring cheese and peppers to room temperature. Drain cheese with slotted spoon, but do not remove rosemary. Place one round on Radicchio or Bibb lettuce leaf and surround with peppers.

Makes 6 servings.

*For best results use only extra-virgin olive oil.
Contributed by Regina Schrambling

My Friend De's Pickled Peppers

Lovely to look at, even better to eat.

> 12 red or green bell (or other) peppers
>   juice of 1 lemon
> 2 large garlic cloves, sliced thin
> 2 Tablespoons vegetable oil
> 1 Tablespoon olive oil
> 1 teaspoon salt

Place peppers in broiler or on burner on top of stove until skins blacken and peppers get soft. Remove skins, leaving stems on, and leave peppers whole. Mix together the lemon juice, garlic and oils. Stir to mix well. Add salt. Mix. Spoon over peppers. Cover and refrigerate overnight.
Serve cold.

HINT: The best peppers are shiny, thick-fleshed and firm; medium to dark green or bright red are freshest and at their peak.

Fried Bell Peppers

> 5 bell peppers
> 2 Tablespoons oil
>   salt
>   freshly ground pepper
> ⅓ cup flour
> 1 egg, beaten

Preheat oven to 450º(F).

Roast peppers in a 450º(F) oven for about 15 minutes, or until they peel easily.

Peel, remove seeds and cut into slices. Place slices in a dish and add oil, salt and pepper. Let stand for 30 minutes.

Drain well and dry with paper towels. Roll slices in flour, dip in beaten egg, and fry in hot oil until golden brown.

Serves 4.

Potato Souffle

8 ounces cream cheese
2 eggs
1 small, diced onion
2 Tablespoons flour
2 cups mashed potatoes
1 cup milk
  salt
  freshly ground pepper
¼ cup grated Parmesan cheese and ¼ cup
  seasoned bread crumbs or 3½ ounces can
  french fried onions

Preheat oven to 300º(F).

Add cream cheese, eggs, onion and flour to potatoes that have been mashed with milk. Beat on low until blended. Turn mixer to high speed and beat until light and fluffy. Add salt and pepper.

Pour into greased 9" souffle dish or round baking dish. Sprinkle with cheese/bread crumb mixture, or onions.

Bake at 300º(F) for 35 minutes.

Serves 4 - 6.

Hilde's Potato Salad

An old Alsatian family recipe.

> 3 *pounds white potatoes*
> ¼ *pound bacon, chopped into small pieces*
> 2 *teaspoons sugar*
> *freshly ground pepper*
> *salt*
> ⅓ *cup cider vinegar*
> ¼ *cup chopped celery*
> ¼ *cup chopped onion*
> 1 *cup heavy cream, at room temperature*

Boil potatoes, then peel and slice. Cook bacon pieces. Do not pour off grease. Remove from heat and add sugar, pepper, salt, and vinegar. Stir until sugar is dissolved.

Pour mixture over potatoes, and add celery and onion. Keep at room temperature.

One-half hour before serving, pour cream over potato mixture; toss well. Let potato salad sit at room temperature, because if mixture is chilled the sauce will not be absorbed. Potatoes can be made ahead and brought to room temperature before completing.

Serves 6.

HINT: Purchase only firm, unblemished potatoes; never ones with sprouts. Store potatoes in a cool dry place—not the refrigerator, and not near your onions or the potatoes will get mushy and the onions will sprout!

Sweet Potato Pecan Pie

 1 9" unbaked pie crust
 1 cup cooked, mashed sweet potatoes
 1 Tablespoon butter
 ¼ cup firmly packed light brown sugar
 1 Tablespoon vanilla
 ¼ teaspoon cinnamon
   pinch of freshly grated nutmeg
1/8 teaspoon allspice
 ¼ teaspoon salt
 2 eggs, beaten
 2 Tablespoons sugar
 1 Tablespoon whipping cream
 ½ cup chopped pecans
 ¾ cup sugar
 2 eggs
 ¾ cup dark corn syrup
1½ Tablespoons melted margarine
   pinch of salt
   pinch of cinnamon
 2 teaspoons vanilla

Preheat oven to 300º(F).

Combine potatoes, butter, brown sugar, vanilla, spices, beaten egg, sugar, and cream and beat at medium speed until mixture is smooth. Spread on bottom of pie crust, and sprinkle with pecans.

Combine ¾ cup sugar, 2 eggs, corn syrup, melted margarine, salt, cinnamon, and vanilla and beat well. Pour over pecans.

Bake at 300º(F) for 1½ hours. Cool. Serve with whipped cream.

HINT: Sweet potato skins range in color from light tan to brownish-red. Generally speaking, the darker the skin, the sweeter and moister the flesh. Select small to medium sized sweet potatoes that taper at both ends. Store in cool, dry, dark place.

Jack-O'-Lantern Compote

1 *small pumpkin*
2 or 3 *large tart apples, peeled and chopped (about 2*
cups)
1 *cup yellow raisins*
¾ *cup chopped pecans*
⅓ *cup water*
⅓ *cup sugar*
1 *teaspoon lemon juice*
1 *teaspoon grated lemon peel*
¼ *teaspoon cinnamon*
freshly grated nutmeg to taste

Preheat the oven to 350º (F).

Wash and dry pumpkin. Cut off top, leaving a nice slice for lid.

Place pumpkin in a large shallow baking dish, and scoop out all seeds. (These may be baked separately for a nutritious snack.)

Combine remaining ingredients in a medium saucepan, and bring to a boil.

Pour apple mixture into pumpkin, and cover with the lid.

Bake for 45 to 55 minutes, or until apples are tender.

When serving, be sure to scoop out some of the pumpkin meat. This compote can be served hot or at room temperature.

Serves 6 - 8.

Pumpkin Walnut Bread

1¾ cups cooked pumpkin
1½ cups light brown sugar
  1 stick melted butter or margarine
  3 eggs, lightly beaten
  5 cups flour
  2 Tablespoons baking powder
  1 teaspoon cinnamon
  ½ teaspoon nutmeg
     salt
  2 cups chopped walnuts

Preheat oven to 350º(F).

In a bowl, stir together pumpkin, sugar, melted butter or margarine, and eggs. Mix well.

Sift together dry ingredients and stir into pumpkin mixture. Stir in walnuts. Pour the batter into 2 well greased loaf pans, (9⅝"x 5½") and bake at 350ºF for about 1 hour, or until bread tests done.

Cool, slice and serve. Freezes beautifully.
Yields 2 loaves.

Radish and Orange Salad

12 ounces radishes, trimmed
2 Tablespoons sugar
1 - 2 Tablespoons lemon juice
1 Tablespoon orange flower water
salt
2 navel oranges
cinnamon

Shred radishes in a food processor or "grate" with a blender. Allow excess liquid to drain off. Toss with sugar, lemon juice, orange flower water and add salt to taste. Chill.

Peel and slice oranges. Just before serving, arrange all together and dust with cinnamon.

Serves 4.

HINT: Radishes are one of the few vegetables that are never cooked. Their spicy flavor makes a delectable salad. Select uniformly shaped, brightly colored, firm radishes. Wash (and discard tops) before refrigerating.

Spinach-Cheese Squares

1 cup flour
1 teaspoon salt
1 teaspoon baking powder
2 eggs
1 cup milk
¼ pound margarine
½ grated onion
2 pounds spinach, thoroughly washed, and
   steamed for 2 minutes
½ pound grated Cheddar cheese

Preheat oven to 350º(F).

Sift all dry ingredients together. Add eggs, milk, and margarine and mix on low speed of mixer. Add onion and spinach. Blend. Add cheese.

Spread in greased 9"x 13" pan and bake at 350º(F) for 30-35 minutes. Cool before cutting.

Serves 4 - 6.

HINT: The freshest spinach leaves are crisp and dark green. Store loose spinach in crisper, but try to use it as soon as possible for the best flavor and retention of nutrients.

Creamed Spinach

1 *pound fresh spinach, washed, trimmed, with stems removed*
2 *cups rapidly boiling salted water*
2 *Tablespoons margarine*
2 *Tablespoons finely chopped onion or shallots*
1 *Tablespoon flour*
½ *cup heated whipping cream*
1 *teaspoon sugar*
freshly ground pepper
salt
freshly grated nutmeg

Place spinach in rapidly boiling water. Then reduce heat and cover and simmer for about 15 - 20 minutes or until tender. Drain well, and chop fine.

In a large skillet, melt margarine and sauté chopped onion for a minute or two over medium heat. Stir in flour, but be careful not to burn it. Slowly stir in heated cream and sugar. Cook and stir until smooth, then add spinach. Stir and cook for another 3 minutes.

Season to taste with pepper, salt, and freshly grated nutmeg.

Serves 2 - 4.

Sounds-Awful-But-Tastes-Great-Spinach-Strawberry-Salad

10 ounces fresh spinach, washed, stemmed, torn into pieces and dried
1 pint fresh strawberries, cleaned, hulled and cut in half
½ cup sugar
2 Tablespoons sesame seed
1 Tablespoon poppy seed
¼ teaspoon Worcestershire sauce
¼ teaspoon paprika
½ cup vegetable oil
¼ cup cider vinegar

In a large bowl, combine spinach and strawberries.
Place all the ingredients for the "dressing" in a blender, except the oil and vinegar. Turn on blender and pour in oil and vinegar. Blend until thick and blended. Drizzle over salad, toss and serve.
Serves 6 - 8.

Spaghetti Squash Salad

You'll need a microwave oven for this recipe.

> 1 *spaghetti squash (3 pounds)*
> ¼ *cup parsley, chopped*
> ¼ *cup olive oil*
> 2 *Tablespoons margarine*
> 2 *teaspoons minced fresh garlic*
> ½ *pound fresh mushrooms, sliced*
> 3 *Tablespoons butter or margarine*
> ¼ *cup grated Parmesan cheese*
> *salt*
> *freshly ground pepper*

With a knife, pierce the skin of squash in several places to allow steam to escape while cooking. Place whole squash in microwave oven and cook on HIGH for 15 minutes, turning once or twice. Remove from oven and let stand 10 minutes. Or, cut in half lengthwise, remove seeds and place cut side down in pot with 2" of water. Cover and boil 20 minutes.

In a small bowl, place parsley, olive oil, margarine and garlic. Cook on HIGH for 1 minute (or heat in pan on medium heat on your stove). Set aside.

Sauté mushrooms in 3 tablespoons butter or margarine. Cut squash in half lengthwise and remove seeds and membrane. With a fork, gently pull spaghetti-like flesh away from sides of outer skin. Combine squash with mushrooms. Pour butter mixture over vegetables and sprinkle with cheese, salt, and pepper. Stir and serve.

Serves 4 - 6.

Summer Squash Pancakes

3 cups grated squash
½ teaspoon salt
3 Tablespoons fresh parsley, minced
½ teaspoon garlic powder
¾ cup grated Parmesan cheese
1 egg
¾ - 1 cup flour
¼ teaspoon baking powder
dash of pepper

Combine squash, salt, parsley, garlic powder, cheese, egg, flour, baking powder, and pepper. Mix to make a fairly thin batter.

Drop by spoonsful onto an oiled griddle or skillet. Cook until brown on bottom. Turn and cook another minute.

These may be reheated in the oven after freezing.

Serves 8.

Squash Pudding

This may be served hot or cold.

> 2 *pounds yellow squash*
> 3 *eggs, beaten*
> 3 *Tablespoons flour*
>   *salt*
> 2 *Tablespoons sugar*
> ¾ *cup milk*
>   *dash Tabasco*
> ¾ *stick margarine, melted*
> ¾ *teaspoon baking powder*

Preheat oven to 350º(F).

Cook squash in steamer over boiling water, covered, for about 8 minutes, or until soft enough to mash. Drain well and mash.

Add beaten eggs, flour, salt, sugar, milk and Tabasco. Mix well. Add melted margarine and baking powder.

Pour into lightly greased cake pan or ovenproof dish and bake at 350º(F) for about 50 minutes.

This can be served with a tomato sauce if desired.

Serves 6 - 8.

Garden Squash Casserole

A favorite of my friend Diane.

   12 *small yellow squash, cut in 1" cubes*
    1 *bunch of green onions*
    2 *Tablespoons butter*
    1 *can cream of celery soup*
    2 *whole eggs*
  ⅓ *cup bread crumbs*
    1 *Tablespoon Worcestershire sauce*
       salt and pepper
       grated cheese
       cracker crumbs mixed with butter

Par-boil squash in salted water just until tender. Drain and set aside.

Sauté green onion tops (use the long stems for garnish) in butter. When soft, remove from heat and stir in celery soup. Add eggs, bread crumbs and seasonings. Combine with drained squash.

Put in a buttered casserole, and cover with grated cheese and additional bread crumbs or cracker crumbs kneaded with butter.

Bake at 375º(F) for 30 to 45 minutes. (Note: Romano cheese that you grate yourself is especially tasty in this recipe.)

Serves 8 - 10.

HINT: Look for 3" - 6" long yellow squash, which is 4" in diameter or less. As these squash are picked at an "immature" stage, their rind and seeds should be tender and edible. Keep only 3 - 4 days before using.

Tomato Mustard Pie

1 8" or 9" unbaked pie or pastry shell
3 Tablespoons Dijon Mustard
1 pound fresh ripe tomatoes, sliced
2 eggs
½ cup heavy cream
  salt
  freshly ground pepper
½ cup grated Gruyere or Swiss cheese

Preheat oven to 350º(F).

Brush the bottom of the pie shell with Dijon mustard. Spread evenly. Place the tomatoes in the shell in an overlapping arrangement.

In a small bowl, mix together eggs, cream, salt and pepper. Stir to blend well. Pour egg mixture over tomatoes. Sprinkle with grated cheese.

Bake at 350º(F) for 30 - 40 minutes or until custard is set. **Serves 4 - 6.**

HINT: Tomatoes from your garden are the best (and they're so easy to grow!) If you need to speed their ripening, wrap in a brown bag or newspaper and store at 65º(F). Don't settle for those mealy, pinkish-yellow supermarket varieties!

Cherry Tomatoes Stuffed with Crabmeat Salad

1 pint cherry tomatoes, washed and dried
1 pound lump crabmeat, picked over and cartilage
   removed
   freshly ground pepper
   salt
   Dijon Mustard to taste
   dash of Tabasco sauce
⅓ cup (or more) mayonnaise

Using a grapefruit spoon, hollow out tomatoes, and let
stand for about 30 minutes, upside down, on paper towel.

Mix together crabmeat, pepper, salt, mustard, Tabasco,
and mayonnaise. Adjust seasoning to taste. Fill tomatoes
with above mixture and refrigerate until serving.

Serves 6 - 8 as an appetizer.

Good-For-Ya-Chili

½ pound dried kidney beans
½ pound dried pinto beans
1 large onion, finely chopped
2 ribs celery, finely chopped
3 cloves garlic, minced
1½ teaspoons paprika
1½ Tablespoons chili powder
½ teaspoon cumin
1 teaspoon oregano
2 cups chopped tomatoes
1 Tablespoon tomato paste
   dash of Tabasco
   freshly ground pepper
2 Tablespoons soy sauce

Place beans in a pot with water to cover, and bring to a boil. Cook for 2 minutes, then cover and let stand for 1 hour, off the heat. Drain, saving ¾ cup of cooking liquid.

Combine all ingredients in a large pot, bring to a boil, reduce heat and simmer covered, for 5 hours. Add more water if needed and correct seasoning.

Freezes well.

Serves 4 - 6 (Triple recipe for a crowd.).

HINT: Tomatoes are very fragile. The best ones have a uniform good color, with firm flesh. Handle gently. Use as soon as possible. If you must store them, do so at room temperature and be sure they are all standing on their bottoms. The "shoulder" area around the stem is easily bruised. Refrigeration diminishes their flavor.

Marinated Zucchini

1   cup bottled chili sauce
3   Tablespoons freshly grated Parmesan cheese
2   Tablespoons red wine vinegar
2   Tablespoons olive oil
    dash of garlic powder
½   teaspoon oregano
2   Tablespoons lemon juice
    salt
    freshly ground pepper
6   medium zucchini, sliced about 1/8" thick

Combine chili sauce, cheese, vinegar, oil, garlic powder, oregano, and lemon juice. Beat well to mix. Season to taste with salt and pepper.

Toss zucchini slices with dressing. Cover and chill 6 - 8 hours or overnight, turning several times.

Serves 6 - 8.

HINT: What would summer be without zucchini? Select tender-skinned, small, firm squash, and use it as soon as possible for the best flavor and quality.

Vegetable Pull-A-Part Bread

From my dear friend Sheena in Michigan.

> 1 stick margarine or butter
> ½ cup chopped red pepper
> 1 cup chopped zucchini
> ½ - 1 cup chopped onion
>   salt and pepper to taste
> 3 cans refrigerated biscuits, (10 each), cut in half horizontally
> ½ cup crisp crumbled bacon
> ½ cup freshly grated Parmesan

Preheat oven to 350º(F).

In a skillet, melt margarine and saute red pepper, zucchini and onions, salt and pepper, until they are soft.

Grease an angel or bundt pan and put in a layer of the biscuit halves, followed by a layer of half the vegetables. Cover vegetables with a layer of half the bacon and then cheese.

Repeat layers, ending with a layer of biscuits.

Bake in a preheated 350º(F) oven for 35 - 45 minutes. If desired, bread can be sprinkled with additional Parmesan the last 10 minutes of baking. Unmold and serve.

Serves 10-12.

Note: Use your creativity and try other vegetables in place of the zucchini.

Curried Zucchini Soup

  1 *medium onion, sliced*
  1 *Tablespoon powdered ginger*
  2 *or more Tablespoons curry powder*
     pinch of saffron
 ¼ *teaspoon chili powder*
  2 *large potatoes, peeled and sliced*
  7 *cups of water*
1½ *pounds zucchini, sliced*
  1 *teaspoon dried basil*
 ½ *cup low fat yogurt*

In a large pot, over medium heat, cook onion in ¼ cup water for 3 minutes. Add ginger, curry, saffron, chili powder, and cook another 3 minutes.

Add potatoes and stir well. Then add 7 cups of water, stir, cover, and simmer for 30 minutes. Stir in zucchini and basil, cover the pot, and cook another 20 minutes.

Puree the soup and strain it. Add yogurt and serve.
Serves 6.